CCSS **Genre** Realistic Fiction

W9-AKX-392

Essential Question
What experiences can change the way you see yourself and the world around you?

SNAP HAPPY

by Diana Noonan
illustrated by Amerigo Pinelli

CHAPTER ONE

CAVE LAKE— AGAIN!

"Have a great time, guys! I'll give you a call when I get home."

Mom's car crunched away down the leafy drive toward the lake. Gran and Gramps waved good-bye and then turned to Madison and me.

"What do you two want to do first?" they asked, as if everything were new and exciting and we hadn't been coming to their cabin at Cave Lake every year since we were little. "Fishing? Canoeing? How about a hike to the waterfall?"

Madison and I tried to look interested. Our grandparents are cool, and we weren't treating their suggestions with disdain. It was just that we wished we were back in the city, having fun with our friends. The city could be noisy and crowded. However, we could go to movies or ball games, and there were always free concerts in the parks. My best friend was going to a science day camp. Madison's friend was taking art classes at the museum, and our neighbors were actually having a sleepover party at the zoo.

Yet here we were, stuck at Cave Lake—again. If only Mom were free, we would have more choice in the matter. But as Mom always reminds us, the start of summer vacation is a super busy time for librarians. There was no way she could get time off to take us anywhere.

I think Gran noticed that Madison and I didn't look interested in the activities she had suggested because after we had finished unpacking, she handed us a pamphlet.

"*What's Up at Cave Lake?*" said Gramps, reading over our shoulders.

It was on the tip of my tongue to say something smart like, "Nothing's ever up at Cave Lake. It's as boring as ever," but I kept my lips firmly zipped.

"It's a competition for kids," said Gran. She pointed at the pamphlet. "Look, it tells you what you have to do to win the mystery prize."

3

"Prize?" Madison said, looking more closely at the pamphlet. "It says here that you have to explore activities around Cave Lake that are new and exciting. Then you have to ..." She stopped. "Oh, you need a camera. Whatever you discover, you have to take a picture of it. I didn't bring my camera. Did you bring yours, Tim?"

I shook my head. "Gramps, Gran, do you have a camera we could use?" I asked.

"Oops, I left it at home," said Gramps. Gran sighed as if leaving things behind were something Gramps did quite a lot. I must have been a teeny bit interested too, because the idea of not being able to enter was kind of disappointing.

"Tell you what, though," he added, "my old friend Bert Baker is bound to have one."

"Bert Baker?" asked Madison.

"He lives by himself on the other side of the lake," said Gran. "He's a very quiet man, but my word, is he smart!"

"I'm sure Bert could loan you a camera," said Gramps. "Luckily, it's Monday, so he'll be coming into town to have lunch with his daughter. I'll give him a call and see what we can organize."

"But there is nothing new or exciting to do at Cave Lake!" I whispered to Madison once we were out of earshot.

"I know," said Madison. "Nothing, with a big, fat capital N!"

We looked down at the lake, a crystal bowl shimmering in the sunlight. Its edges were fringed with dark trees, and here and there, you could just make out the roofs of cabins. It was pretty—really pretty, especially with the bare, rocky mountains poking up behind, so I felt a bit guilty about wanting to be somewhere else. It wasn't really that Cave Lake was boring. It was just that we had done everything there was to do and seen everything there was to see. In fact, so had everyone else who had ever been here more than once.

"You know what?" began Madison.

"What?" I asked.

"I can't think of one new, exciting activity anywhere in this whole place. Hiking, canoeing, fishing—that's it! That's Cave Lake. There *is* nothing else to do."

Below us, a duck quacked. Something plopped into the lake, and ripples spread out across the water. I looked at Madison and nodded. She was 100 percent right.

CHAPTER TWO

ON THE HUNT

The next morning, with Bert Baker's camera and a picnic lunch but not a lot of hope, Madison and I set out to see what we could photograph.

"Think of yourselves as detectives!" called Gramps as we stomped down the path toward the lake. "And don't get your socks wet!" said Gran. She always says that when we go anywhere near the water.

When we were halfway along the lakeside trail to town, we saw a family pushing a couple of plastic buckets along the surface of the water. Every now and then, they stopped and looked down into them as though they were really interested in something.

"Does that count as a new, exciting activity?" asked Madison.

"It counts as serious weirdness," I replied. By the time we'd reached the family, they had come ashore and were delighted to tell us what they'd been doing.

"We made them ourselves!" said one of the kids, holding up an orange bucket. "We cut out the base and glued in clear plastic."

"Look," said his dad. "When you hold the base of the bucket on the surface of the water, you can see right to the bottom."

"There are water bugs everywhere and sometimes fish too!" said the other kid.

Madison took the pamphlet out of her backpack to help explain to the family what we were doing, and the next minute, I was taking their picture.

"That was a fluke, a lucky chance," I said to Madison. "It won't happen again."

Before long, though, we had Bert Baker's camera out again—and again! First there was an art class, right on the edge of the lake, with easels and paint palettes and everything. The teacher said she held it at Cave Lake every summer. Sometimes she took the students into the woods and sometimes to the mountains. This year, the class was at the edge of the lake.

Snap, snap, snap, went the camera. The teacher even gave us tips on taking arty shots of just the palette of paints and the lake.

"Thanks!" we called as we headed off along the trail. "Thanks so much!"

Then Madison and I photographed an eco-tour group of birders heading onto the water in kayaks, a man smoking fresh fish fillets on a home-built smoker, and rock climbers rappelling down a bluff. By this time, we were feeling really pleased with ourselves.

Cave Lake, meanwhile, began to feel like a whole new place. Madison and I were talking as if we were the managers of some big tour company telling everyone to come to the lake for their vacation! We even started thinking that we might actually win the competition. Before long, we were trying to guess what the mystery prize might be.

We just had to win, and when we discovered an outdoor karate class, we knew we were going to. I mean, who would ever guess that there was a karate class at Cave Lake?

Madison got out the camera and started snapping photographs like crazy. She must have taken about 20 shots—some of them superb—until we made a surprise discovery. On the other side of the lawn, someone else was taking shots of the karate, too. Our hearts sank. We weren't the only ones in the competition.

The boy holding the camera waved and then came over with his kid sister. They were as pumped up as we were about the competition, and before her brother could stop her, the kid sister had blurted out just about everything they'd photographed. I couldn't believe it. They'd discovered exactly the same activities as we had, plus a couple extra! What's more, they'd seen some other kids scouting around with cameras, too.

Suddenly it seemed as if Madison and I had no prospect of winning anything. There might be a whole lot more to do at Cave Lake than we had ever realized, but that did not mean we would win the competition.

"What now?" asked Madison when the boy and his sister had gone.

I shrugged. "I guess we just keep focused on hunting and snapping. We have six more days before the competition ends."

I tried to sound positive, but deep inside I didn't feel that confident. As the week went on and we met more and more groups of kids out snapping pictures, I almost gave up. It wasn't until the last day of the competition, after we had downloaded our million and one pictures onto the "What's Up at Cave Lake?" Web site and were returning Bert's camera, that I began to think differently.

CHAPTER THREE

HIDDEN TREASURE

"No one's home," said Gramps after we had knocked on Bert's door. "His car is here, though. I guess he must be tinkering around in his shed."

Gramps was right. As soon as we pulled up outside the shed, Bert appeared. In his hands was the strangest camera I had ever seen.

"It's an 1891 Henry Clay," said Bert when he noticed me staring at it. "Are you interested in cameras?"

I didn't want to say no, but before I could open my mouth, Bert was beckoning us inside. If I hadn't been interested in cameras before, I sure was now. Bert's shed was absolutely full of them. I was totally stunned by the variety. Some were as big as a TV. Others had lenses at the end of long, concertina-like cloth tubes with black capes that hung down at the back like curtains.

Madison was busy looking at the old photos that were hanging around the walls.

"Are these pictures of Cave Lake?" she asked.

"Yes, sirree," said Bert. "Every one of 'em."

We gazed up at women in long dresses, holding frilled umbrellas and sitting in wide wooden boats. Children in overalls and straw hats held fishing lines that were twice as long as the ones Gramps kept in the cabin basement.

One of the photos showed the mountains behind the lake, but there were no trees in sight.

"That was taken after the big fire in 1933," said Bert. "It burned almost every tree around the east side of the lake."

We spent a long time looking at Bert's cameras and photos. I liked the way everything was neatly arranged on shelves or in groups. It was like being in a museum. When I looked at it like that, it was as if a light suddenly went on in my head.

"Mr. Baker?" I asked, my heart beating loudly in my ears. "Is this … is your shed kind of like a museum?"

Bert chuckled. "I guess you could call it that," he said.

Madison must have figured out what I was thinking because the next minute I heard her say, "Tim, you're a genius!" Then she said to Bert, "Would you mind if people came to take a look around here?"

"Not at all," said Bert. "I get a group coming in every now and again. I wouldn't mind a few more, but I guess not too many people know about it."

I looked at my watch. We had 20 minutes left to enter more photographs in the competition. "Would you mind if we took some pictures of all this?" I asked. "We're looking for new and exciting activities to do around Cave Lake. It's for a competition we've entered."

"I don't see why not," replied Bert.

Five minutes later, Gramps was driving us back into town to the library so we could use the computer to download our extra photographs.

So that's how Madison and I ended up winning the "What's Up at Cave Lake?" photograph competition! One kid had found a man who made wood sculptures using his chainsaw, and someone else had discovered cheese-making classes in the school cafeteria, but Madison and I were chosen as the winners. It seemed no one else had any idea that Bert Baker had the most incredible camera and photo museum just on the other side of the lake.

As for our mystery prize, we won a scenic flight over Cave Lake in a helicopter. It was totally awesome—but not as cool as what we ended up doing for the rest of the vacation. As soon as our win was reported in the newspaper and people heard about the camera museum, Bert's phone didn't stop ringing. Absolutely everyone wanted to visit his shed.

"I need a hand over there," said Bert one evening when he came over to visit Gramps. "Someone to help show the visitors around. You think you can lend me those grandkids of yours to help out?"

Madison and I didn't need any persuading. In fact, we asked Mom to let us stay at the lake longer than we had planned. Helping Bert was so much fun that we didn't want to leave.

"Sounds as if you have a new perspective on the place," laughed Mom when we called her on video-chat. "What brought about this sudden transition?"

"Helping Bert at his museum," I told her. "It's great. He's even teaching us how to use some of the old cameras."

"And that's not all," added Madison. "Tomorrow, Tim and I are going to our first karate class!"

"What?" asked Mom.

"Karate," I said. "Come up to the lake and try it for yourself. Or you could pick one of our other fantastic discoveries. Cave Lake is ready and waiting for you!"

Respond to Reading

Summarize

Use the most important details from *Snap Happy* to summarize the story. Your graphic organizer may help you.

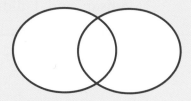

Text Evidence

1. What features help you identify *Snap Happy* as realistic fiction? **GENRE**

2. Compare the settings of the lake and the city. How does the difference explain Tim and Madison's responses early in the story? **COMPARE AND CONTRAST**

3. How does using comparisons in the surrounding sentences help you figure out the meaning of *fluke* on page 7? **CONTEXT CLUES: COMPARISON**

4. Write to describe how Bert's shed as a setting contrasts with the natural setting of Cave Lake. **WRITE ABOUT READING**

Compare Texts

Read about a boy who discovered something new about his musical abilities.

DRUM ROLL FOR JUSTIN

Justin's new friend, Mario, sat at the kitchen table eating warm cupcakes and talking about music with Justin's mom and dad. He was chatting about stuff like rhythm and beat, the types of things Justin had never been able to fathom.

Almost every day, Justin wished he were musical like the rest of his family. He had tried out lots of different instruments and had taken keyboard, violin, guitar, clarinet, and cello lessons. None of them really worked for him, not even the easy old recorder!

The fact was he just could not seem to master anything, which was so weird when the rest of his family members played almost every instrument you could imagine.

Justin sighed and looked around the room. Reminders of music were everywhere. The curtain fabric was printed with musical notes, and framed music certificates hung on the walls. Music stands clustered in a corner of the room, and a guitar rested on its stand beside the piano. In a family such as his, Justin's lack of musical ability sometimes made him feel as if he were an alien.

"Anyway," he heard Mario say at last, "I'd better get going to orchestra rehearsal." He turned to Justin. "Do you still want to come with me and wait until I finish? Then we can head to soccer practice together."

Justin picked up his sports bag and followed Mario out the door. When they reached the orchestra's rehearsal room, Justin said he would wait outside, but Mario invited him in.

"You might like what you hear," he said.

A few minutes later, Justin was witnessing something totally unlike any orchestra performance he had ever attended. Musicians pounded African skin drums with the palms of their hands while dancers leaped as if the floor were made of red-hot coals. The stage's painted backdrop of dry brown-and-orange African hills captured the mood perfectly. Justin wanted to clap and dance as the music's energy coursed through his body.

Justin was still tapping out the rhythm as Mario jumped down off the stage and picked up his sports bag.

"Cool drumming, Mario," Justin said. "Would it be okay if I sign up for lessons?" Justin smiled to himself. He wasn't unmusical after all! He had just been waiting to find the right instrument.

Make Connections

What was it that changed Justin's perspective on his musical ability in *Drum Roll for Justin*?
ESSENTIAL QUESTION

Compare the experiences that changed Madison and Tim in *Snap Happy* and Justin in *Drum Roll for Justin*. How are they similar and different? **TEXT TO TEXT**

19

Focus on
Literary Elements

Figurative Language Writers are using figurative language every time they describe something by comparing it with something else. There are many ways they can do this. Some examples include using metaphors, similes, personification, or onomatopoeia.

Read and Find On page 3 in *Snap Happy*, Tim says, "I kept my lips firmly zipped." The writer uses a metaphor by comparing keeping quiet with the action of a zipper.

On page 5, the author describes the lake as "a crystal bowl shimmering in the sunlight." This is a metaphor.

On page 19 in *Drum Roll for Justin*, the author uses a simile to describe the dancers leaping "as if the floor were made of red-hot coals."

Your Turn

Find three examples of figurative language from the text. Make a sketch to show what each might look like if it were used literally. Turn your sketches into full-color illustrations that can help remind everyone to use figurative language in his or her writing.